D1527580

HOLOCAUST BIOGRAPHIES

Heinrich Müller
Gestapo Chief

Mark Beyer

THE ROSEN PUBLISHING GROUP, INC.
NEW YORK

Published in 2001 by The Rosen Publishing Group, Inc.
29 East 21st Street, New York, NY 10010

Library of Congress Cataloging-in-Publication Data

Beyer, Mark.
Heinrich Müller: Gestapo chief / by Mark Beyer.
p. cm. — (Holocaust biography)
Includes bibliographical references and index.
ISBN 0-8239-3376-8
1. Müller, Heinrich, 1900—Juvenile literature. 2. Nazis—
Biography—Juvenile literature. 3. Holocaust, Jewish
(1939–1945)—Juvenile literature. 4. Germany—Politics and
government—1933–1945—Juvenile literature. 5. Hitler, Adolf,
1889–1945—Juvenile literature. 6. Germany. Geheime
Staatspolizei—Juvenile literature. [1. Müller, Heinrich, 1900–
2. Nazis. 3. Holocaust, Jewish (1939–1945) 4. Germany—
politics and government—1933–1945.] I. Title. II. Series.
DD247.M74 B49 2001
363.28'3'092—dc21
                                                    2001000350

Manufactured in the United States of America

Contents

Introduction   5

1. Professional Policeman   14

2. Hitler and the Nazi
   Rise to Power   23

3. Müller and the Gestapo
   at Work   44

4. World War II and the
   "Jewish Question"   63

5. The Attempt to Kill Hitler   78

6. Hitler's Final Days   86

7. Müller's Escape   93

   Timeline   101

   Glossary   104

   For More Information   107

   For Further Reading   109

   Index   110

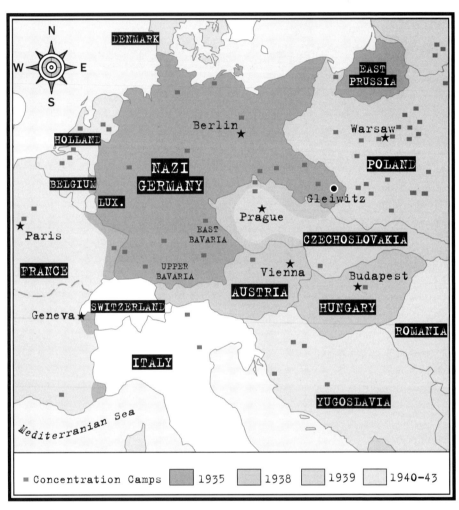

▪ Concentration Camps	1935	1938	1939	1940-43

Hitler's dictatorial leadership under Nazism fortified his vision of a "Greater Germany." During WWII, his goals were to secure living space, or *Lebensraum*, and to unite all the German-speaking countries of Europe, eliminating twelve million people he deemed unfit in the process.

Introduction

In August 1939, Gestapo chief Heinrich Müller sent six of his agents across Poland's border to the German town of Gleiwitz. Quietly, the agents were told to wait for a signal and then attack the radio station in the town. They were ordered to dress in Polish army uniforms during the attack and to use the radio station to broadcast a speech by a Polish-speaking German. This attack was the first part of a two-part plan implemented by Germany to instigate a conflict with Poland.

Müller telephoned his men at noon on August 31. The signal was given. That night the six Gestapo agents broke into the radio station. The broadcast given on that fateful evening by a Polish-speaking German called for the Polish army to attack Germany at once. Afterward, the Gestapo agents fired several shots and left. Their mission had taken less than half an hour.

The second part of the plan took place later that night. Approximately twelve German criminals (posing as Poles and dressed in Polish army uniforms) were forced to gather in an area along the German-Polish border. Gestapo agents shot the criminals and left their bodies on the ground. Then the area was made to look as though Polish troops had attacked German troops. Müller referred to these doomed individuals with little emotion and called them *konserven*, or "canned goods." Müller had lied to the prisoners. He had told them that they would be taking part in a film, and that they would be pardoned for their participation.

The next morning, German and foreign newspaper reporters were brought to the scene. They took pictures of the attack and the dead criminals dressed in Polish uniforms. The press would tell the German people and

German general Blaskowitz (left, center of the table)
presides over the official surrender of the Polish army
in a railway car at the Skoda Motor Works, near Warsaw.

the world that Poland had attacked Germany. The German people would be angry. They would call for war. Hitler and the Nazis didn't wait for the people, however. On September 1, the German army attacked Poland. The Nazis claimed they were defending Germany. The Gestapo plan had worked.

The Gleiwitz border incident wasn't the only staged attack against Germany. Similar actions, all of which involved Müller, took place in other cities, such as Beuthen and Hindenburg. These attacks gave Hitler his pretext for the Polish invasion of 1939.

Britain and France didn't believe the Nazis' story about Polish attacks on German troops. They declared war against Germany and World War II (1939–1945) began. The Nazis didn't care if the world didn't believe their false attack plan. Adolf Hitler, the Nazi leader, cared only that the German people believed that Poland had attacked Germany. With the German people's support, Hitler could go to war with the world.

It may come as a surprise to learn that the German police helped the Nazis plan this fake attack. We learn from an early age that police officers are hired to protect citizens against crime. Police patrols allow people to walk the streets without fear of being robbed or killed. Criminals fear the police because they know the police help send criminals to jail.

When the police become criminals themselves, however, there is no law that protects citizens. This is what happened to German citizens under Nazi rule. During the years 1933–1945, German citizens feared the German police. The Gestapo, Germany's secret police organization, was given power to arrest and jail anyone whom they thought was against the Nazi government.

Heinrich Müller was a police detective in the German state of Bavaria for fifteen years before the Nazis came to power in 1933. Later, as Gestapo chief, Müller helped the Nazis control Germany. Many people and groups wanted to take power away from the

This photo of SS troops on parade is from an album
given to Adolf Hitler by an unknown SS officer.

Nazis. Communists, underground (secret) groups, and many regular citizens wanted to end the Nazi government. They saw the Nazis as evil, violent criminals. Many Germans believed the Nazis would use the German army to try and take over Europe.

Müller's job as Gestapo chief was to employ any methods possible to locate these people and put them in jail or kill them. Anyone who was against the Nazi government became a criminal. Hitler and the Nazi commanders allowed the Gestapo to work above the law. The Gestapo had the right to go anywhere and do anything to keep the Nazis in power. This power made Gestapo officers dangerous. They began to break the laws that they were supposed to uphold.

People were pulled off the street and were never seen again. Homes were broken into and citizens were put in jail for saying things against the government. News reporters were jailed for writing anti-Nazi articles. Political party offices were robbed or burned down.

Jews were jailed and beaten on the streets. Thousands of teachers, writers, lawyers, and politicians were thrown into concentration camps to silence their anti-Nazi opinions. These individuals were known as dissenters—people who resisted the Nazis and their rise to power.

The Gestapo had spies all over the country. They paid citizens to incriminate dissenters. Germans began to live in fear. They didn't know whom they could trust. They could not trust the police. They could not trust their neighbors. People began to wonder if they could trust their own friends. Once the people lived in fear, the Nazis were in control.

Although Gestapo chief Müller rarely tortured, interrogated, or even visited the concentration camps where prisoners were held, he did uphold the government orders that sent thousands of people to their deaths. (According to some accounts of World War II, he was even more directly involved in the

extermination program than SS
[Schutzstaffel] officers Heinrich Himmler or
Reinhard Heydrich.) Prior to becoming head
of the feared Gestapo, Müller was one of the
most influential officers of the SS, which at
that point was already deeply involved in the
extermination of the Jewish people. Unlike
many others, who committed suicide or were
tried and convicted of unthinkable war
crimes, Müller escaped unharmed from
Germany after the war. This is the story of a
cold, calculating man with little conscience,
who spent much of his adult life diligently
working to uphold the laws that Hitler's
madness created.

1. Professional Policeman

Heinrich Müller was born on April 28, 1900. His father worked in local government in Bavaria, a southeast German state. The Müller family was lower-middle class. They worked hard and earned enough to live. The Müller family went to church, and Heinrich was raised Catholic. He would remain religious throughout his life.

Müller completed the German equivalent of American high school. Then he went to technical school and trained as an aircraft engine mechanic. In June 1917, Müller joined the German army and fought in World War I (1914–1918). His mechanical training got him sent to a fighting airplane group on the western front in April 1918. Only seven months remained until the end of the war.

Müller was a bright young man. His commanders noticed his intelligence and within two months he was made an officer. He learned to fly airplanes and fought in air battles until the war ended. His flying skills won him the Iron Cross First and Second Class. For any officer, these medals were special honors. They were given only to pilots who shot down enemy planes and showed courage in battle.

Müller retired from battle after an airplane accident. He had injured his leg and would walk with a slight limp for the rest of his life. By that time, he had earned the Bavarian pilot's badge. Müller was just eighteen years old.

Policeman in Munich

Müller went home to Bavaria after the war, and soon moved to the capital city of Munich. Once there, he joined the Munich police force in 1919. He worked as a junior assistant while

The German Police and the People

Even before the Nazis, the German government had control over its citizens' lives. In America we are used to traveling freely throughout the country. Germans could not travel freely in Germany before the end of World War II. People in Germany had to carry citizenship papers with them at all times. When they moved to a different home, they had to tell the police where they were living. Germans also had to inform the police when they changed jobs and for whom they worked.

Political groups had to register with the government and give the police a list of all of their members. Such laws forced many people and groups to work in secrecy. This made the policemen's job more difficult. The police had to learn how to work secretly themselves. When the Nazis took over in 1933, the German police already knew how to control people.

he studied for his police entrance exams. After passing his examinations, Müller became a police officer.

Little is known of Müller's professional career during the next ten years. It is safe to say that he effectively learned police methods. Müller never took another job in his life. Even as Gestapo chief, he was a policeman and did police work.

In 1924, Müller married Sophie Dishner. Three years later, they had a son, Reinhard. A daughter, Elizabeth, came much later, in 1936. She was born with Down's syndrome (medically called mongoloid in those days) and this caused conflict between Müller and his wife. But during the 1920s, the Müllers were living happily in Munich.

By 1929, Müller was promoted to police secretary. He worked in Section VI of the Bavarian state police. This unit investigated communists, underground groups, and other violent political groups working in Munich in the 1920s. As already noted, many of these groups wanted to overthrow the German government. It was the job of policemen like Müller to stop them.

Information is a powerful tool for the police. Müller learned what happened at political meetings. He also read what these groups printed and passed around to citizens. This kind of information, however, was not enough to stop crime and violence. Müller needed to know what the political leaders were planning. He had to find out about secret and public meetings, street marches, and scheduled fights before they happened. He also had to know if one group or another was going to try to overthrow the government.

Müller used spies to learn what political groups were doing. The police used people in all positions to get information. Some of what the police learned was false, told to them as lies. Lies about a fight or march could throw the police off the track of a real plan. Yet, in spite of all the useless

information and lies, enough truth was
learned to do significant harm to the political
groups, preventing any takeover of the
government. All of this police work was great
training for Müller. He learned how spies
acted, what they wanted, and what they
needed to succeed. He also learned how to
keep them from succeeding. This education
would help him greatly when the Nazis took
over the government.

The Nazi Party

By coincidence, Munich was also home to Adolf
Hitler in the 1920s. Hitler was a member of the
newly formed National Socialist Workers' Party.
Political groups had a legal right to exist under
the democratic Weimar government, that had
been formed in 1919, after World War I and the
signing of the Treaty of Versailles. The Weimar
government was very liberal and allowed for
elected leaders and politicians, a bill of rights,
and suffrage for all people. The democratically

19

elected Reichstag (German legislature) had
members from several different political
groups, including the Nazi Party. By contrast,
the Nazis favored authoritarian rule. Nazism
grew out of the poor economic conditions in
Munich (and all of Germany) after World War I.
The Nazi Party battled politically against both
the Weimar government and the German
Communist Party.

Adolf Hitler stands in a public square with
supporters at a *Deutscher Tag* (German Day) rally
in Nuremberg in 1923.

Nazi Putsch

In 1923, Hitler and the Nazis tried
to overthrow the Weimar government.
On November 8, Hitler decided to
seize his opportunity to take
action. During a rally to honor
Gustav von Kahr, the newly appointed
Weimar leader, Hitler decided to
surround the beer hall where they
were meeting with storm troopers
(Sturmabteilung), or SA troops. The
troops also took over Bavarian
government offices in Munich. They
planned to march on Berlin within
days. Munich's green police ended
the revolt, or putsch, by shooting
into the crowd and scattering the
army as it marched in the streets.
Sixteen Nazis were killed and many
were injured, but Hitler emerged
unharmed. Later he was captured and
put on trial for treason. After
being found guilty, he was sentenced
to a five-year prison term. The
Nazi Party was outlawed. But Nazism
appealed to some Germans, and when
Hitler was released from prison
early, after serving only nine
months of his sentence, the Nazi
Party became active again. In nine
years, it would become a huge force
in German politics.

As early as the 1920s, many Germans feared what the Nazis would do if they ever controlled the German government. In fact, Müller's father-in-law published a newspaper that printed articles against the Nazi Party movement.

2. Hitler and the Nazi Rise to Power

Adolf Hitler rose to power and became Germany's chancellor in 1933. In 1932, his political party, the Nazi Party, won more than 13 million votes and 230 of the 670 seats in the Reichstag, becoming Germany's second-largest political party. This allowed Hitler to force the Weimar government in Germany to include him in the government. The Weimar leaders didn't respect Hitler or the Nazis. They thought both were using the German people to gain political control. They were correct. They could not, however, ignore the Nazi Party.

The Nazis began to gain political power in Germany in the 1920s after Germany had been defeated in World War I. The Versailles treaty, the peace agreement that Germany signed, forced the government to pay 132 billion gold German marks to the winning countries. These countries included Britain, France, and the United States.

The Versailles treaty also limited the size of Germany's army and took away land that Germans had always considered part of their country. The German people thought the demands that the treaty imposed were too

Officials sign the Treaty of Versailles in France on June 28, 1919. The treaty limited the expansion of the German army and made Germany pay restitution to the Allies.

harsh. They were humiliated and their morale was low. They were also angry with the Weimar government for signing the treaty.

The government could not help the people. France and Britain wanted Germany to pay for having started the war. Germany suffered financially. Germans also suffered from mass unemployment after the war. Between 1918 and 1924, the German economy collapsed. German money became almost worthless. People were starving. They began to look for help.

In the 1920s, conservative political parties developed from this crisis. Many parties wanted to end the Weimar government. Others cried for revenge against Germany's enemies. As head of the Nazis, Hitler promised jobs to the German voters. He also promised the voters that Germany would again become a European power. Hitler told the German people that their government was swindling them. Many liked what they heard from Hitler. His enthusiasm gave the Nazi Party its strength. The voters began electing Nazi Party members to the Reichstag. Hitler saw his chance to become the leader of Germany.

The 1932 elections gave the Nazis enough seats in the Reichstag to make their leader part of the government. Hitler demanded a top role. The Weimar leaders thought that they could control Hitler. They gave him the powerful job of chancellor in 1933.

Hitler's Promises

To hold onto power, Hitler needed to get rid of his enemies. He also needed to make some very powerful friends. First, the Nazi Party passed laws that removed power from the Reichstag. These laws began to drain power from all of the Nazi's political enemies. Next, Hitler needed the German army to support him as Germany's new ruler. He and Nazi leaders met with army generals. Hitler told them that as leader, he would never try to control the army. The army would be independent of political rule. The generals believed Hitler's promise.

Supporters of Adolf Hitler march through the
streets of Berlin two days prior to the
presidential election of 1932.

Finally, Hitler needed help from the leaders of German industries. He promised the owners of German factories that they could keep their businesses if they helped Germany become a European power again. They would help the German economy by hiring Germans to make weapons and other war materials.

The president of Germany, Paul von Hindenburg, died on August 2, 1934. By law, Hitler should have called for a presidential election. Instead, he ordered a plebiscite, or a direct vote, from the German people. They were to vote on whether they wanted Hitler to continue running the government. The plebiscite vote was 90 percent in favor of Hitler leading the German people. Hitler and the Nazis were in complete control of Germany. Hitler declared "emergency" power by law when he and the Nazis initiated the Enabling Act that gave him dictatorial leadership abilities. He placed the country under military rule. The Nazi Party gave him the name "Führer," or leader.

Nazi Propaganda Begins

Hitler outlawed all political parties except the Nazi Party. The Nazis took over all national media outlets, including newspapers, magazines, radio stations, and film companies. It was in this way that Hitler could begin to utilize methods of propaganda—information, ideas, or rumors used to spread a cause—to influence people's opinions about the Nazi Party. Hitler was already an expert at using false information to manipulate the German people, since he was first put in charge of propaganda for the Nazi Party in 1920. It was then that he had realized the need for a vivid symbol to distinguish the Nazis—the swastika. In 1933, Hitler put Paul Joseph Goebbels in charge of Nazi propaganda.

German citizens were given only the information that Hitler and the Nazis wanted them to hear and know. This propaganda was used to spread lies about communists, foreign countries, and German Jews.

Magazines printed stories of Jewish treachery. Radio stations broadcast false stories about communist plots against the German government. Thousands of people were arrested and placed in concentration camps. Thousands more were murdered.

Many Nazi laws suddenly made criminals of average people. One day, they were citizens living within the law, and the next day, they

A German soldier forces Poles and Jews to stand in line with their arms raised.

were outlaws. The Nazis needed a police force that could enforce the new laws and arrest the growing number of "criminals."

In 1933, Hitler ordered Hermann Göring to build a new police force. This police force would work in every city, town, and village in Germany. The police officers would be loyal only to the Nazis and Hitler. Göring soon created the *Geheime Staatspolizei* (secret state police) out of the regular police forces that had served Germany for many years. This police force was known forever after as the Gestapo.

The Gestapo's job was to find and jail enemies of the new Germany, or the Reich. The only way that Hitler and the Nazis could fool the people into believing Reich propaganda was to quiet those people who were against them. Laws could make speaking against the government illegal, but the police had to enforce these laws. Too many people and groups wanted to end Hitler's rule before it began. The Nazis needed the Gestapo to control the people so that the government could spread its lies.

Hitler's Vision

Hitler wanted Germany's citizens to believe in his Nazi government. He wanted Germans to fear Jews, communists, and foreigners so that they would hate these groups. Once Germans began to hate, they would want to fight. Hitler wanted Germans to fight for him and for the fatherland of Germany. He had plans to expand German territory. Hitler wanted Germany to have more *Lebensraum*, or "living space."

After a few years of hearing lies, the German people began to believe the Nazis. They began to hate the communists and foreign governments. They hated the Jews most of all. Hitler had poisoned the German people's minds about Jews. He blamed Jews for all of Germany's problems. A book that he published in 1925, written while he was imprisoned, told all about Jewish "wrongs" against Germans and Germany. In *Mein Kampf* (My Struggle), which was dedicated to his friend and cellmate, Rudolf Hess, Hitler blamed Jewish industrialists for Germany's losing World War I. He thought Germans should own businesses, not Jews. He blamed Jewish bankers for causing the worldwide depression. Worst of all, he blamed Jews for trying to pollute "pure" German blood by marrying non-Jewish Germans. Hitler called pure Germans "Aryans" and said he would protect Aryans from the Jews. After becoming Führer, Hitler directed all of his hatred toward the Jews. The German people believed him. They tolerated his hatred and began hating Jews themselves.

The Nuremberg Laws

Hitler believed that only Aryans with pure German blood were "true" Germans. He believed that Germany's people had been compromised by the introduction of outsiders such as Poles and Jews into their society. To enforce these racist beliefs on the German people, he instituted a law for the protection of German blood and German honor, which prohibited intermarriage between Jews and Germans. This law was one of many laws—known as the Nuremberg Laws—that limited the civil rights of Jews.

The Nazis also passed laws that allowed the government to take over Jewish businesses. The government then handed over these businesses to Germans. Jews

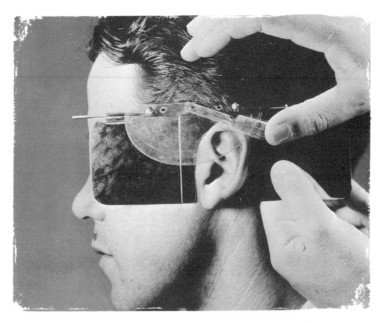

German doctors actually measured peoples' facial features to determine if they were Jewish.

working in the German government were fired. Jewish teachers were removed from colleges and schools across the country, and soon after, Jewish students could not attend college. Then Jewish children could not go to school. By 1938, 235,000 German Jews had fled the country in fear.

The Gestapo arrested Jews, along with communists and many teachers, and placed them in concentration camps. Many were murdered. Others were released from the camps after many months. Many had all of their possessions taken away. The Gestapo was beginning to gain enormous power and wealth while it spread fear throughout the country.

The Night of Broken Glass

By November 1938, Germany's Jews became more than merely ostracized or conspired against. Crimes against Jews became more violent and barbaric.

A Polish Jew and outcast named Herschel Grünspan, who had been frustrated by Germany's ill treatment of his family, burst into the German embassy in Paris and fatally shot Ernst von Rath, the Reich's third secretary. At this news, principal Nazi officers were outraged and determined to severely punish the Jews who remained in Germany.

Nazi anger reached a peak on November 9–10, 1938, known as *Kristallnacht,* or the "Night of Broken Glass" when hundreds of synagogues were broken into or were razed by fire. Jewish-owned businesses and private homes also were destroyed in large numbers, and thousands of Jews were arrested. Some Jewish men were thrown into frozen rivers. Their property was stolen, their money and valuables were looted, and their wives and daughters were assaulted. The worst crimes occurred in the cities of Berlin, Leipzig, and Nuremberg. In all, more than 1,200 Jewish-owned buildings were either set on fire or

On the morning after *Kristallnacht,* local residents
watch as the Ober Ramstadt synagogue is destroyed
by fire.

were completely destroyed that night, and thirty-six people died. Many others were physically assaulted and injured, some seriously, and had no hope of receiving medical care or other assistance. Those Jews who survived were left penniless and emotionally violated.

Müller, directly involved in *Kristallnacht*, sent direct orders to his Gestapo officers to arrest 20,000 to 30,000 wealthy Jewish men on that night and immediately thereafter. One of the key messages from Müller came at midnight that very evening:

"Actions against Jews, especially against their synagogues, will take place throughout the Reich shortly. They are not to be interfered with. So far as important material exists in synagogues this is to be secured by immediate measures. Preparations are to be made for the arrest of about 20,000 to 30,000 Jews in the Reich. Above all, well-to-do Jews are to be selected. Detailed instructions will follow in the course of the night."

Why the Gestapo Was Formed

Hitler and the Nazis finally had the power that they wanted. Hitler knew that every dictator has enemies. He needed an organization that could find these people and either jail them or kill them.

The Nazis had a private army that had helped them spread terror and win votes over the years. The *Schutzstaffel,* or SS, could not become a reliable police group, however. They had no experience with police matters. Most of the SS troops were effective only for fighting. Hitler needed professionals who knew police methods. He needed men who knew how to work secretly. He needed a group that could use people to get information.

Hermann Göring had developed a secret police force in Prussia in 1933, which was the model on which the Gestapo was formed. In 1934, Göring handed over control of the

Gestapo to Heinrich Himmler, head of the SS. Himmler formed the Gestapo with some of his own best officers. Himmler ordered Reinhard Heydrich, a smart but brutal man, to find the right people for the jobs that needed to be filled. Heydrich used common sense and quickly brought

Senior SS officials meet at Gestapo headquarters in Munich. They are, from left to right, Heinrich Müller, Franz Huber, Heinrich Himmler, Reinhard Heydrich, and Arthur Nebe.

professional policemen from around the country into the SS.

Heydrich remembered Heinrich Müller's political police group in Munich. Müller was an expert on communist groups. Heydrich knew that Müller had formed a good spy organization in Munich. Müller was also known as a professional who got results. He was exactly the kind of policeman that the Nazis needed to eliminate the communists. Heydrich brought Müller and some of his men to Berlin to join the Gestapo.

Nazi Party members knew who Müller was. They were shocked when he and the men from his political police bureau were hired to run the Gestapo in 1933. Even at this point in his early career with the Nazi government, Müller was known to have a vicious drive toward perfectionism. He was often described as a man of limited imagination who would have blindly followed the orders of Hitler or any other leader.

Gestapo Control

Many Germans wanted to disobey Hitler and the Nazi Party long before the end of the war. Many tried. They could not overthrow Hitler or the Nazis, however. Those who tried were under constant fear of being arrested by the Gestapo. Hitler's new government had fooled so many Germans that too few were left who knew the truth about what was happening to Germany.

Fear is how any evil government controls its people. Armies and police forces are used to keep people silent. Those who speak against the government are put in jail or killed, or sometimes mysteriously disappear. When hundreds—and then thousands—of people disappear, the rest of the people are terrified to speak. They hear nothing, they see nothing, and they say nothing. This is how the Nazis and the Gestapo took control in Germany and held power.

Müller's Gestapo officers used counter-espionage (spying on secret groups working to overthrow the government) to control Germans who wanted to rid Germany of Hitler and the Nazis. The Gestapo worked secretly. Sometimes they wore plain clothes so people wouldn't know they were police. They paid spies and informers for information. Knowing something about every citizen gave the Gestapo great power. For this reason, records were kept on every German citizen and political group. Information about people and their actions helped the Gestapo do their work.

Quite often, however, people knew exactly who the Gestapo officers were. Gestapo officers worked in every German factory and company. They were in the military, in churches, and in each government office. These officers listened and watched as Germans worked. Talk about the shortage of butter could bring a harsh warning from a Gestapo officer. The Gestapo presence was enough to silence people.

3. Müller and the Gestapo at Work

Müller rose quickly in the Gestapo. He was a smart, hard-working professional. His knowledge as a police investigator and an expert in counter-espionage made his work important to the Gestapo's early success.

The Gestapo received official recognition in 1936 as an independent national police force. This was also about the same time that the Gestapo began to administer law within the concentration camps. Müller was hired as a Gestapo officer because he was an expert spy and he knew how to employ espionage—the practice of using spies to gain information—to control all types of organizations. The Gestapo got their people into important positions and then weakened those in charge. This is how

Hitler and the Nazis had worked during the 1920s, and they continued to use information as a means of control—to bribe, scare, or kill.

Müller Rises to Gestapo Chief

In 1934, within a year of working for the Gestapo, Müller became head of Department II, which investigated political groups and was considered the core of the Gestapo. As the head of this department, he would watch left-wing radicals, Marxists, and communists. Two years later, he was promoted to *Kriminalrat,* or senior police officer. In 1939, Müller became *Reichskriminaldirecktor,* or director of police. Müller was the Gestapo chief. He controlled twelve different departments. As head of the Nazi government's secret police, Müller was the fourth most powerful person in Germany. He could have anyone arrested—even his boss—if that person was caught trying to overthrow Hitler.

Many members of the Gestapo were ordinary German
citizens. These Gestapo agents were arrested and
incarcerated in Belgium in 1944.

Müller took his job seriously. It never seemed to matter to him that he was working for a madman who was trying to take over the world. To Müller, his job was to ensure that the laws of his country were enforced and the orders of his superiors were carried out. Müller's blind obedience and his fanatic devotion to duty made him an extremely dangerous man.

Gestapo Methods

The Gestapo worked within every part of German society. Even before Müller became Gestapo chief, networks of citizen informers were growing in number around the country. To this end, listening posts recorded every international telephone call. The mail was watched. Files were kept on every citizen. Müller had access to all of this information.

Müller was a great student of the Soviet Union's secret police forces. For many years, he studied how the Soviets controlled Russian citizens. Müller used aggressive Soviet methods to make the Gestapo even more effective.

The Gestapo was not the standing police force in Germany. Every city, town, and village had its own police force to protect its citizens from crime. (The Gestapo often questioned the local police to get information, but they always worked alone.)

Why did the Gestapo work alone? Why did the Nazis need a "secret" police force? The answer to these questions, of course, is control. The Nazi government needed to control power. To do this, it needed to control its enemies. Most of its enemies were Germans, so all Germans were considered suspects. The Nazis, therefore, needed to control the German people.

Müller oversaw each department's daily operations, including its network of agents and spies, from his office in Berlin. He worked closely with each department head to ensure orders from the Nazi high command were enforced. He saw that every order from Heydrich and Himmler was carried out as effectively as possible. Sometimes, however, Müller directed an interrogation himself. He also traveled throughout Germany to oversee operations against Soviet spies working in Germany and occupied countries such as Poland and Italy.

Spy Networks

There were not enough Gestapo agents, however, to watch 80 million Germans. The greatest number of agents the Gestapo ever had was 25,000. That meant there was one agent for every 1,300 people. There was no way that any secret police force could control everyone if they were outnumbered 1,300 to one. So how did the Gestapo control Germans?

The Gestapo used a network of spies to gather information. The spy networks were made up of paid and unpaid informers. Müller called them his "V" people. They worked in business, government, and the military, and they lived in every city, town, and village.

Many informers gave the Gestapo information because they thought it was their duty as Germans. Other informers had a grudge against something or someone. Some informers were reliable, and others were useless. The Gestapo, however, could not work without the V people. They rarely could get the kind of information that V people got for them every day. Without informers, the Gestapo could not work; without the Gestapo, Hitler and the Nazis never would have lasted for long.

With the help of his informers, Müller controlled the fate of almost every German citizen. People could not speak on the streets without wondering who was listening. They could not speak on the telephone without wondering whether their conversations were being recorded. When people went to work, Gestapo agents were watching. Everywhere they went, Germans wondered if the person sitting next to them was a Gestapo agent.

Fear of being jailed or killed makes people obey the law. Many Germans who did not like the Nazis did nothing to overthrow them. How could they do nothing? Simply knowing that an organization to overthrow the Nazis existed could get a person arrested and tortured. The Gestapo knew that if they could control information and the spread of information, then they could control the people.

Being watched makes people defensive. When they fear that they are being watched, they don't trust anyone. When trust disappears between people, they are alone. This became Nazi Germany: Each person was alone, fearful, and defenseless.

Mass Arrests

Nazi enemies included teachers, political opponents, the clergy, Jews, and others. The Nazis feared these people because their ideas were different from Nazi ideas. Nazi opponents wanted the freedom to write, speak, and teach about all subjects. The Nazis wanted Germans to think only

To control the spread of anti-Nazi sentiment, the
Gestapo ordered that thousands of books be destroyed.

nationalistically—about Germany and helping Germany become a world power again. They passed hundreds of laws that took away civil rights. Other laws banned books and public protests. Some laws banned teaching certain ideas in classrooms and using certain books.

Müller kept political opponents quiet by arresting them. The Gestapo arrested rebellious citizens. Germans were forbidden from speaking, writing, or reading about opposition to the Nazis. Anyone caught doing such things was arrested. New Nazi law controlled protesting, certain ideas, and membership in political groups and made anyone engaged in those types of activities a criminal.

Imagine you are a newspaper reporter writing about the Nazis, and the next day a law is passed that makes it illegal for reporters to write about the Nazis. Suddenly, you are seen as a criminal. The Gestapo arrests you for doing your job. It doesn't matter that yesterday your job was legal; today it is illegal and you are arrested for your crime.

Laws banning certain jobs and types of work allowed the Nazis to arrest teachers, doctors, lawyers, priests, rabbis, politicians, newspaper and radio owners, and others. The Nazis couldn't take the chance that ideas against their government would reach all Germans, so they arrested anyone who was a potential opponent.

At first, many Germans who wanted help from the Nazi leadership went along with these laws. But after they came to power, the Nazis wanted to make sure Germans didn't change their minds. In just a few years, Müller and his Gestapo agents had terrorized the German people. Soon it was too late for Germans to do anything against the Nazis. Too many had been silenced or fooled into believing Nazi propaganda.

Müller and the Communists

When the Nazis outlawed the Communist Party, Müller arrested anyone who belonged to

Dulling German Minds

The Nazis didn't want young Germans to have the chance to learn about ideas that were not approved by the Nazis. If they did, young Germans might not want the Nazis to run the government anymore. The Nazis wanted young people to work and fight for them. They didn't want young people wasting their time reading about things that would not help Germany become a world power. Laws banned many books, including volumes about philosophy, literature, religion, and psychology. The Gestapo helped organize book-burning ceremonies. Some of the books that were burned included works by the German writers Goethe and Schiller; the literature of Mark Twain, Henry David Thoreau, and Charles Dickens; the Bible and other religious writings; and Sigmund Freud's books on psychology.

communist cells (small groups). Those not immediately arrested began to meet secretly. Müller's early years in the Gestapo were spent forming a spy network to gather information about communist cells in Germany.

Müller needed to learn which cells were still active, so he used his V people to learn who belonged to which cell. Müller and his Gestapo agents waited for a meeting of the

Prinz-Albrecht Strasse 8, the headquarters of the Gestapo and the Reich security main office.

cell, allowing them a better chance to capture more people. The Gestapo broke into beer hall cellars, company storage rooms, and even bedrooms to catch communists. Thousands of political opponents were arrested in just a few years. Many were murdered immediately. The others were sent to prison labor camps.

Interrogations

The Gestapo questioned every person who was arrested. Müller learned many of his interrogation methods from the Soviets. The Soviets, however, arrested people to make them confess to their crimes. Müller and the Gestapo didn't want confessions. It didn't matter to them whether the person was guilty. Müller wanted information from prisoners about people and political groups working against the Nazis. He wanted to know what these people were doing and where they were. Information was important, not a confession of guilt.

Most people arrested, however, had little important information to give the Gestapo. In fact, many people were questioned and then released. They were merely people whom the Nazis feared as enemies. A quick release did not mean that prisoners were treated well, however. The Gestapo regularly beat anyone who was arrested.

The Gestapo quickly learned if a person had something important to tell them. If a citizen had committed a crime worthy of being in jail, he or she was warned and released. Usually, anyone who was picked up by the Gestapo and released would never do anything to get arrested again because they feared death.

Müller's Interrogation

Only one description of Müller's interrogation method exists. This came from a British intelligence agent named Captain Best. He was caught in Holland in 1939, after an assassination attempt on Hitler, and told this story:

"Müller was a dapper, exceptionally good-looking little man, dressed in imitation of Adolf Hitler, in a gray uniform jacket, black riding breeches and top boots. He started his 'snort' immediately when he entered and, as he walked towards me, increased the pitch and the volume of his voice with great virtuosity. He managed to get right up close to me before his vocal cords tore into shreds. 'You are in the hands of the Gestapo. Don't imagine that we shall show you the slightest consideration. The Führer has already shown the world that he is invincible and soon he will come and liberate the people of England from the Jews and plutocrats such as you. It is war and Germany is fighting for her existence. You are in the greatest danger and if you want to live another day, you must be very careful.'

"Then he sat down on a chair in front of me and drew it up as close as possible, apparently with the intention of performing some mesmerizing trick. He had rather funny eyes which he could flicker from side to side with the greatest rapidity and I suppose that this was supposed to strike terror into the heart of the beholder."

Beating Prisoners

Many arrests began with beatings. In fact, beatings continued up until the time of questioning—and after, if the person didn't talk.

Although Müller seldom tortured anyone himself, he ordered others to assault prisoners. The Gestapo wanted to wear away people's will to fight, and beatings weakened them easily. By the time prisoners were questioned, they were in such pain and fear that most told the Gestapo anything they wanted to hear.

Prisoners were put in a room after being beaten. Müller yelled and threatened prisoners with torture and death if they did not speak. Most people talked. If Müller didn't believe what a prisoner said, he would order the beating to continue. Prisoners who wanted to protect their friends were tortured or killed.

Gestapo agents observe a Polish resister who has
been beaten to death.

Torture

The most common form of Gestapo torture
was flogging, or beating with a stick.
Sometimes the bottoms of the feet were
flogged, causing great pain and swelling. Other
times, the back of the legs or the lower back
was flogged. Flogging gave prisoners the most
pain without breaking bones or causing death.

When prisoners didn't talk, stronger torture methods were used. Müller lied about Gestapo torture and claimed that torture methods included only flogging. Survivors of Gestapo torture said that the Gestapo also burned people, held their heads under water, put them in ice-cold water for hours at a time, and used electric shock. Some prisoners were murdered with a bullet to the back of their heads.

Stories of arrest and torture became common on Germany's city streets. People thought that only enemies were tortured, but soon stories began to circulate about ordinary citizens dying in Gestapo jails. Many Germans wondered how this could be true. How could the Nazis be doing this to their fellow citizens? But ordinary German citizens also felt it was much too late to do anything, even if they had the courage to try. The Gestapo had eliminated every possibility of protest.

4. World War II and the "Jewish Question"

In 1939, Germany attacked Poland and World War II began. For the next six years, the German army fought against the world and tried to take over all of Europe. The Germans defeated many European countries. The German army occupied these countries while the war raged on. In the east, the Germans fought against Russia. In the west and south (North Africa), they fought against Britain and later, the United States. Not until 1944 did the German army begin to lose battles against the Allies (Britain, France, the Soviet Union, the United States, and more than sixty other countries). The Allies began pushing the Germans back from all directions. Less than a year later, the war would be over and Germany would be defeated.

Inside Germany during the war, many Jews and enemies of the Nazis died. Special concentration camps became work camps filled to capacity with prisoners. Jews, communists, and other criminals were forced to work in factories to support Hitler's war machine. Most of these people were worked to death, dying from starvation or exhaustion. Others were shot for stealing food or for working too slowly. Life in the camps was brutal and horrific.

After 1938, the Gestapo used their files to find Jews, count them, and send them to labor camps. This plan was an answer to the "Jewish question," the issue of what Germany would do with its Jews. Concentration camps were built to hold Jews and other prisoners. Later on, in the occupied territories, the Gestapo used SS troops to section off parts of cities into ghettos where Jews were sent. The SS guarded the Jews inside these ghettos until more camps could be built.

European Jews and the Secrecy of War

Germany went to war six months after Müller became Gestapo chief. Poland was attacked in September 1939. The Germans defeated Poland in eight short weeks. Poland's Jews were then under Nazi control. Three million Polish Jews, only a portion of the European Jews that Hitler wanted to kill, were at the mercy of Hitler. There would be no Nazi mercy.

Hitler and the high command decided to send Germany's Jews east, into Poland. Most German Jews already were dying in German concentration camps. Others still lived under heavy restrictions in their own towns. Heydrich headed the Jewish relocation plan and later the extermination plan. He had almost a dozen concentration camps built inside Poland. Each camp could hold more than 100,000 Jews. Jews were worked to death in these camps. Many died of disease or were murdered by guards. Mass extermination would come later.

The Final Solution

Under the cover of war, Hitler wanted to work Jews to death using them for slave labor, such as working in factories or building roads. Others were put to work digging holes just to fill them up again. Thousands of women and children were murdered because they were not strong enough to work. Thousands more were too old

During the Holocaust, the Nazis murdered 12 million people, half of them Jews.

and weak to work. These individuals were lined up next to deep holes in the earth and shot. Their bodies were buried in mass graves.

The war helped Germany kill its Jews and the Jews that had been rounded up in Poland, and the other countries it occupied. The Germans defeated France, Hungry, Greece, and the Balkan countries before Hitler attacked the Soviet Union. As the Germans occupied these countries, they rounded up the Jews who lived there and sent them to concentration camps or ghettos. A year after Poland was defeated, Hitler decided it was time to start murdering every Jew that Germany could find. Little news came into German lands for people to hear, and little news left for the world to know what was happening. Hitler felt it was safe to begin his program of murder.

In 1941, Müller delivered the orders to round up thousands of European Jews—orders known as the notorious *Nacht und Nebel Erlass* (Night and Fog Decree). These laws were directed primarily against western countries and enabled the Gestapo to arrest individuals and make them "disappear," wiping out all record of their existence. At this time, the first concrete plans for mass genocide had appeared, organized at the conference at Wannsee in January 1942.

By 1942, Hitler and his generals decided on the Final Solution—to kill all the Jews in Europe by gassing them and burning their bodies in ovens. Special camps were built for this purpose alone. They were called death camps. Under the secrecy of war, the Gestapo sent six million Jews to their deaths by working them to death or gassing them. Nearly six million non-Jews were also killed.

Müller assured Himmler that he could increase the number of prisoners in the German camps. At this point, Müller promised to deliver 45,000 additional forced laborers within six weeks, or before the end of January 1943. He was said to have been obsessive in nature, and, like Hitler, zealous and forthright in his opinions about the need for mass extermination of the Jewish people. Müller never did these things himself. In fact, there's little evidence that Müller ever visited a concentration camp. He passed on this order of extermination, and many others like it, to his people to enforce. Müller knew exactly what was happening to the Jewish people and to other enemies of the state. He understood that he was helping Hitler to complete one of the most horrific genocides that the world had ever known. It has been said that in his hands, "mass murder became an automatic, administrative procedure."

There are numerous accounts of Müller's monstrous nature. Conversations between Müller and officers that he sent to observe the Nazis' killing methods were, at times, brutally cruel. Once, when Müller sent Adolf Eichmann, an SS "Jewish expert" and administrator of the entire genocide, to witness 1,000 Jews being gassed in sealed buses, Eichmann was so affected by the action that he forgot to time the procedure. Müller coldly castigated him afterward about his distraction, reminding him of his Nazi duties.

Knowing that he was sending people to their deaths didn't seem to bother Müller. He sat in his office and received orders from Hitler, Himmler, and Heydrich. When orders were issued to send Jews to work camps (and later, to death camps), Müller would tell his people, "The Reichsführer wishes this done. See that the order is carried out." This became the defense that all German generals and soldiers used after the war: "I was only doing my duty. I obeyed orders."

Hiding Their Crimes

The Nazis tried to hide what they were doing to Europe's Jews. Before 1941, they buried their victims in huge pits. As the war turned against them, the Nazis forced Jews to dig up the decaying bodies that had been buried so that the Nazis could better hide what they had done. By then the death camps were killing

Inside the Gestapo teletype room, field agents
relayed news about suspected subversives.

Jews by the thousands every day. Dead bodies
were burned in ovens and the ashes spread in
the surrounding forests.

The Nazis were careful record keepers. They
had records of citizens, people arrested,
interrogations, tortures, people in jail, and
every person sent to a concentration camp.
Near the end of the war, in March 1945, Müller
ordered that every Gestapo record be destroyed

to cover up all their crimes: unlawful arrests and imprisonment, torture, murder, and mass murder of Nazi enemies and Jewish men, women, and children. Some records survived and were found after the war. Heinrich Müller's signature is on many orders that sent people to their deaths, including entire railcars filled with Jews. Müller sent millions to their deaths using only his signature.

Resistance Groups and Foreign Agents

As Germany defeated Poland, then France, and, finally, much of Europe, Müller had to fight against resistance groups and foreign agents. The Gestapo did not officially work outside of Germany. Müller, however, had agents in most countries that Germany occupied. Every country defeated by Germany had a civilian population to control. The Gestapo had to show each occupied country that it would not tolerate rebellion.

Müller knew that many civilians in the defeated countries would fight against the German army. These were ordinary citizens caught in war. They wanted to help their country kick out the Nazis. They resisted Nazi occupation by setting up groups to hurt Nazi battle plans, although opponents of Nazi rule feared jail or murder if they spoke out. Later in the war, secret groups such as the White Rose began writing about Nazi war crimes. Members of the White Rose saw the Nazis destroying Germany. They printed leaflets and left them at universities to warn people about the government. The Gestapo searched for members of the White Rose for months. Their members eventually were caught and executed for speaking against the Nazis.

Thousands of people belonged to secret resistance groups in France, Italy, Spain, and Greece. They were in cities and in many towns. They sabotaged railroad tracks, blew up Nazi ammunition warehouses, and assassinated Nazi generals. These were Müller's worst enemies.

Müller often traveled to Italy, France, and Greece to investigate resistance sabotage. When he traveled to Paris in 1942, he met with General Karl Heinrich von Stuelpnagel because of complaints about resistance sabotage attacks. Müller had these words to say about the meeting: "The conference ended with my comments that if these people could not be controlled, they were

Members of the French resistance derail a German train carrying supplies through the Alps.

best interned, deported, or shot, whichever
solution seemed to be the best."

Unlike many Germans, however, foreign
resistance groups would not give up their
fight against the Nazis. Müller's Gestapo
agents captured and executed hundreds of
resistance fighters. Gestapo actions against
the resistance didn't matter, though. For
every person they captured and killed,
another would take his or her place.

Communist Agents

Before and during the war, Müller was
constantly looking for Soviet spies in
Germany and the occupied countries.
What he had learned from studying the
Soviet methods, he used to locate Soviet
spies. The Soviets had a huge spy network
inside Germany (as well as inside the Soviet
Union's allies, Britain and the United States)
and they used it to find out what Hitler and
his generals were planning.

Müller had his own spies working outside the country to reveal the plans of Germany's enemies. It was a game of cat and mouse. Sometimes Soviet spies were caught, and sometimes Müller lost one of his agents to the Soviets. Often, spies worked in the manner of resistance fighters. They would sabotage trucks, railroads, or supply warehouses.

Müller was an expert at "turning" an agent. When a foreign spy was caught, Müller would try to convince him to work as a double agent. The spy would return, but also would give important information to the Gestapo. Sometimes, Müller would turn the agent with threats of torture or death. If the agent turned, he would stay in Germany and help the Gestapo collect Soviet information.

Double agents and turned agents worked for every country during the war. When the Gestapo found that one of its own agents had turned, he was executed immediately. The same happened to spies working for other countries.

Müller often used bribes and promises to turn agents. The promise of money or a better home could turn an agent who was not loyal to his country. Sometimes these promises were kept. Other times an agent was killed after his ability to get information was used. Müller didn't care about double-crossing. He firmly believed that a person who didn't have loyalty to his country did not have the right to live.

5. The Attempt to Kill Hitler

The highlight of Müller's Gestapo career came in July 1944, when he investigated a plot to kill Adolf Hitler—a plan the Nazis referred to as "the 20th of July business."

The Nazis were losing the war. Hitler's generals knew that Hitler would have anyone shot for even suggesting a peace deal with the Allies. Some generals talked among themselves about getting rid of Hitler. A group of six generals and dozens of other army officers plotted to kill Hitler using a bomb planted during a meeting at Hitler's headquarters, the Wolfsschanze.

Colonel Claus von Stauffenberg carried the bomb in his briefcase. He set it beneath a huge conference table where he sat with almost twenty other members of Hitler's high command. Minutes before the bomb exploded, Stauffenberg left the conference room to make a telephone call. At 12:50 PM, the bomb exploded. Four people died. Although the bomb was just ten feet from him, Hitler survived the blast with only minor injuries.

The heavy wooden table protected Hitler from the blast, but the steel vest and steel-lined hat he wore saved his life. Stauffenberg left the Wolfsschanze and took an airplane to Berlin. He had no idea that Hitler had survived.

Müller Leads the Investigation

Hitler asked Müller to personally lead the bombing investigation and questioning of suspects. This was not the first time that Müller and Hitler had met. In September 1931, Müller had investigated the mysterious death of Hitler's niece, Geli Raubal. The hushing of the scandal—and the removal of any witnesses—was Müller's responsibility and he is said to have done it well. Hitler needed someone whom he could trust and who was loyal. Müller had proven himself to be both.

Müller was an excellent policeman. He quickly put together a team of 400 agents to help investigate the assassination plot. Stauffenberg and several Nazi generals were already under arrest. They had tried to take over

Shown here is just one of the many suspected conspirators tried by the infamous Nazi courts for their supposed role in the failed attempt to assassinate Hitler.

the Berlin command office just hours after the bomb blast, and had tried to organize a full-scale revolt. Instead, SS troops broke into the building and shot many of the conspirators. The rest—nearly 7,000 people who were suspected of supporting the conspirators—sat in jail.

Müller questioned everyone who was at the Wolfsschanze and learned of Stauffenberg's movements. Later, Stauffenberg and the surviving plotters were questioned. They gave full accounts of all that they had planned. The plotters were proud of what they had done. They knew that they had tried to save Germany from destruction.

Müller wrote dry, detailed, and thorough reports about his investigation and kept careful notes. When each report was complete, he sent it immediately to Hitler. Hitler had ordered that only he and Müller were to see the reports. Hitler told Müller to keep the documents safe after they had been read. Müller kept his files and evidence hidden and took it all with him when he left Berlin days before the war ended.

The Traitors Are Executed

A huge amount of evidence was found and used to prove the plotters' guilt. Many of the plotters had kept diaries about their roles in the assassination attempt. Interrogation notes gave Nazi lawyers enough evidence to convict every conspirator. Most of them gave Müller dozens of names of people who they claimed had helped in the plot.

Stauffenberg was tried and convicted. He and several other plotters were executed by slow strangulation. In the next few months, more than 200 others were executed for their involvement in the bomb plot.

Hitler was impressed with Müller's work on the investigation. He gave him a signed portrait and awarded him a medal for his service to the Reich.

At that time, Hitler seemed to trust Müller more than most of the generals around him. Of course, he had good reason to distrust his generals. Hitler had been claiming for two years that his generals were traitors. He thought they were losing the war on purpose. If he could have, he probably would have had them all shot. But he still needed them to fight. Müller was closer to Hitler and more loyal than ever before. In the last days of the war, Hitler asked Müller to help him escape from Berlin.

Gestapo Secrecy

Both Hitler and Müller wanted all Gestapo activity kept secret. Of course, they also wanted people to know that some Gestapo officers were among them. Knowing exactly what the Gestapo did and how they worked, however, was to be kept secret. Müller ordered all notes and orders to be destroyed. Once an order from him was read, that paper was to be shredded. Near the end of the war, Müller ordered all Gestapo files destroyed as well. He did not want the world to find out that the Gestapo was sending millions of people to their deaths. The Gestapo orders for secrecy failed, however.

Müller did succeed in keeping one secret, though. That secret included personal information. Few people knew who he really was. He sent orders to his agents and questioned prisoners, but few people really knew him. His secrecy seemed to have been planned.

In March 1945, the Allied armies defeated Germany. The army was unable to fight; the German people were tired of fighting. Nearly every German city was crushed. Hitler left the German people with nothing. Germany had lost everything.

Allied soldiers rescued concentration camp survivors. The survivors then were able to tell the world what had happened inside Germany. Hitler, his generals, and the Gestapo had worked hard to keep their killing a secret, but when Germany was defeated, they could not.

In the last days of the war, Müller disappeared. His wife and two children disappeared also. Many Nazi generals had killed themselves to avoid being caught and punished for their war crimes. Others killed their families, as well. Some were caught after the war and punished for their crimes, but Müller was to suffer neither of those fates.

An official government report stated that Müller had been shot in the street during the last days of the war. A grave, exhumed in 1964, which reportedly contained Müller's corpse, was found instead to contain two corpses, neither of which could be identified as his. In fact, recent documents have been discovered that tell a different story about Müller's end.

6. Hitler's Final Days

Hitler lived in an underground bunker next to the chancellery in Berlin. There, in a small room connected to an office, he ran the last days of the war, meeting with Nazi generals and giving orders.

Hitler's girlfriend, Eva Braun, came to live with him. They were married the night before they committed suicide. Hitler also had with him his pet German shepherd, Blondi, with whom he and Eva would sometimes walk in the gardens. Mostly, Hitler remained isolated in his room, nearly delusional, thinking of ways to win the war that was now completely lost.

Two other Nazi commanders lived in the bunker: Martin Bormann and Joseph Goebbels (minister of propaganda), along with his wife and children. A staff of secretaries, servants, and a cook also lived in the underground bunker.

Hitler and his staff had been living in the bunker for months. By April, everyone knew that the war was lost. Hitler did not want to be taken alive. On April 29, Hitler gave orders to his commanders: After he committed suicide, his body should be taken into the chancellery garden and burned using gasoline. Hitler would not allow his dead body to be used as propaganda by his enemies.

Hitler's Suicide

On April 30, 1945, Hitler used a gun to shoot himself in the forehead. Eva Braun also committed suicide. Both bodies were taken into the garden and were burned by the Nazis.

The complete story took years for historians to piece together. They used interviews of the surviving staff, information from the Russians (whose army marched into

Berlin days later), and a photograph that was taken of Hitler's dead body minutes after his suicide.

Many people, including U.S. Army and British officials, didn't immediately believe the story of Hitler's death. The body was too burned to be recognizable. Dental or medical records that could identify the body were not immediately available. The Russians first claimed they didn't find anything, but months later they claimed they found the body.

Of course, this book is about Müller, not Hitler. Müller survived the war. News of his "official" death only aided his ability to disappear. If enemy armies thought he was dead, they wouldn't bother to look for him after the war had ended.

In 1948, Müller told American officials a different story about Hitler's death. Müller's story includes the final story of his work during World War II. This story was not on historical record until 1995, fifty years after the end of the war.

Müller's Story of Hitler's Death

Müller gave an interview to the U.S. Army's Counter Intelligence Corps (CIC) in 1948. His account tells a different tale of Hitler's last days in Berlin. This story contradicts what historians have accepted as truth for the past fifty years. According to Müller, Hitler called him to the bunker in March 1945. Hitler wanted Müller's opinion about what he should do now that Berlin was going to be lost to the Russians.

As they walked outside in the chancellery gardens, Hitler asked if he should leave Berlin and hide in the mountains (to run the war from there), surrender, or kill himself. Müller said in the interview: "I strongly suggested that [Hitler] not surrender. Why should he? He had fought this long, why give in at the last minute? [Hitler] agreed with that. I also said that if he went to the mountains, the enemy would pursue him without a pause and would finally put him in the same situation he was in now. Namely, to make the same decision a month or six months in the future. That he agreed with, too."

They continued their walk through the garden. Müller wanted to go inside because the temperature was below freezing. Hitler still continued to talk. Müller told the interviewer: "Hitler kept his voice down . . . and began to

Hitler's bunker, located underneath the Reich chancellery, was found by the Russians when they entered Berlin.

discuss the escape idea with me. He was very quick to see things and I do admit that I had given some thought to my own fate. If the Soviets caught me, they would shoot me on the spot and I knew it. Hitler mentioned Switzerland and I spoke against that. The Swiss would never have protected him. He agreed, and then suggested Spain or South America. I suggested Barcelona [Spain] because it was a major port and if Hitler wanted to leave Spain, he could do so much more easily. I had people in Barcelona and I could do this for him. We discussed methods of leaving and how to get to Barcelona."

According to Müller's story, he helped plan for Hitler to leave the bunker on April 22. A car would take him to an airfield south of Berlin. From there, a plane would carry Hitler farther south, and then finally over to Spain. Müller claimed that he last saw Hitler on April 22. Hitler thanked Müller for his help, and had his valet give him a briefcase. Inside was money for Müller to use during his own escape.

Hitler's "Body"

If Müller helped Hitler escape, then whose body lay burned in the chancellery garden? Müller claimed that several days before Hitler's escape, the Nazis brought a man who looked like Hitler to the bunker. He claimed that this "double" looked exactly like Hitler. According to Müller, the double was taught Hitler's mannerisms, and was even used in public a few times in 1944, following the attempt to assassinate Hitler.

The plan was to keep the double in the bunker after Hitler left. On April 30, the double would be shot and burned in the garden, and history would tell that story. Müller said this is how the world was fooled into believing Hitler was dead. Only a few people knew about the double, and they committed suicide a few days after the double was killed. Only Müller was alive to tell the story of Hitler's escape.

7. Müller's Escape

Müller planned to escape from Germany in the last days of the war. He did not want to be captured by any of the enemy armies. He had made plans a year before the war ended to escape Germany and flee to Switzerland.

Leaving Berlin

Müller said the most dangerous part of his escape was getting out of Berlin. The Russian army was just outside the city and bombs were dropping everywhere. Buildings were on fire and streets were ruined.

Müller and his pilot left from the middle of Berlin at 11:00 PM on April 29. The city was dark, and soldiers were fighting in the streets.

By luck, the car was not blown up by a
Russian shell. The plane they would use to
leave Berlin was stored in a suburban area.
Müller claimed that he changed from his
Gestapo uniform to the uniform of an air
force pilot before the airplane was pushed
onto a street for a quick takeoff.

British troops, searching for Gestapo agents
hidden among German soldiers, escort a heavily
veiled informer through the ranks of German POWs
held in Oslo, Norway.

They flew southwest, away from the city. Although Müller feared being spotted by an enemy plane and shot down, he saw only three Russian fighter planes below them, flying northward. He had begun the long flight to Switzerland.

The flight took them over parts of Germany that were occupied by Russians, and Müller feared they would have to make an emergency landing. If the Russians caught him, he faced certain death. The pilot, who knew both Russian and English, listened carefully to the radio. The pilot gave Müller news about enemy movements. Germany was about to lose the war.

Müller and the pilot landed before crossing into Switzerland. They walked across the border with just a backpack filled with clothes and money. They stayed in a house on a Swiss lake. Müller said he slept constantly for two days after the dangerous journey.

Living in Switzerland

Müller brought his family out of Germany months after making his own escape. They lived in a house in the Swiss countryside. The family lived on money that Müller had stolen from the Nazi counterfeit (fake) money program, and he had millions in a Swiss bank account. Also, he had the money that Hitler had given him.

Once out of Germany, Müller never returned, but he had some contacts with former Gestapo officers. From these men, Müller learned that he was "officially" dead. Although in 1946, U.S. Army intelligence reported that there was "no confirmation" of Müller's death, there were rumors that he had been shot in the streets or had committed suicide along with his wife and family. There was even a grave with Müller's headstone in Berlin. There is no evidence that Müller staged his own death, although he had the ability to do so. It was to his advantage that people thought he was dead. He didn't want anyone searching for him.

Müller's Postwar Activities

From the time Müller escaped from war-ravaged Germany, there have been reports and rumors of him working as a security official in espionage around the world, including the Soviet Union, Czechoslovakia, and Argentina. Other reports claim that the U.S. Army CIC discovered that Müller was still alive in 1948. They claim that they made contact with him through Müller's former Gestapo agents. The Americans wanted to talk with Müller. They wanted to know if he would work for the United States.

The war was over, and the United States was concerned about Russian military plans. The Russians had taken over most of the countries of Eastern Europe and weren't going to let them go. The Soviet Union also had many spies inside the United States; some were even working in government offices.

The CIC wanted to talk with Müller. He could give the United States a lot of information about Soviet spy networks. He also could give them the names of hundreds of Soviet spies working in Europe and the United States. If Müller could somehow prove to the United States that he was not a war criminal, they would be able to hire him for his information. If he was a war criminal and news got out that he worked for the Americans, the public (and many foreign countries) would be outraged.

Müller met with CIC agents for more than two months. He was asked about his job as Gestapo chief. He was asked about the Gestapo's role in killing civilians (in all the German occupied countries) and Jews. Müller told them that the Gestapo did no killing. He said that was the job of special SS forces and the camp guards. Müller said the Gestapo was there as a state police force. The Gestapo arrested enemies of the state.

The U.S. government has all of these public records on file in Washington, DC, but many are still considered secret documents.

The Americans decided that Müller had not committed war crimes with his own hands. They believed Müller had put enough distance between himself and the mass killings.

Living in the Caribbean

The Americans hired Müller and moved him to the U.S. Virgin Islands in the Caribbean Sea. He would be safe on American soil, and no one would ever be able to learn that he was still alive. Müller was paid $50,000 per year to help the U.S. government learn about Soviet spies in Europe and America.

Müller was given an additional $1 million for all the files that he had hidden in Germany and had brought to Switzerland. Müller's files had lists of Russian spies and how their spy networks operated. Müller worked for the Americans for many years. It is not known at this time when, or how, Müller died.

Believing Recorded History

We can either believe or disbelieve Müller's story about Hitler. Belief or disbelief often depends on what we know of a person. Müller's interview record shows that he constantly lied about accounts of torture, arrests, executions, and Gestapo control and brutality. He even suggested that less than one million Jews died in concentration camps— and that most of those who died did so from disease, not gassing or execution.

Records and eyewitness accounts clearly tell us that Müller was lying to hide his crimes. Because Müller was a proven liar, his story about Hitler's death is most likely untrue. He wanted a job from the U.S. government. He needed to hide from other governments that were still searching for him. The U.S. government has always denied the charge that it protected Müller.

Timeline

1900	Heinrich Müller is born.
1917	Müller joins the German army in the middle of World War I.
1918	World War I ends.
1919	Müller joins the Munich police force.
1923	Nazi Putsch, or coup, is staged. Adolf Hitler and the Nazis attempt to overthrow the Weimar government.
1924	Müller marries Sophie Dishner.
1925	Hitler publishes *Mein Kampf* (My Struggle), his racist account of Germany's problems after World War I. He wrote it in prison after the 1923 Nazi Putsch.
1931	Müller investigates the mysterious death of Hitler's niece, Geli Raubal.

1932	Germany's elections give the Nazis enough power to make Hitler part of the Weimar government.
1933	The Gestapo, Germany's secret state police, is formed to bring unity to the police force. Heinrich Himmler requests that Müller join.
1934	Müller rises to the head of Department II in the Gestapo, where he is charged with overseeing political groups.
1938	Nazis destroy Jewish businesses and synagogues in an evening of barbaric anarchy. This would forever be known as *Kristallnacht*, or the "Night of Broken Glass."
1939	Müller becomes Gestapo chief, or Reichskriminaldirecktor. Poland is invaded by Germany after Müller's involvement in the Gleiwitz border incident. World War II begins.
1941	Müller delivers the orders to round up thousands of European Jews after the *Nacht und Nebel Erlass* (Night and Fog Decree) is passed.

1942	The Wannsee Conference is held, which allows the Nazis to formalize the Final Solution against the Jews.
1944	Dozens of Hitler's own men try to assassinate him in a bomb plot scheme. Four people die, but Hitler escapes unharmed. Müller leads the investigation.
1945	The Allied armies defeat Germany. Hitler commits suicide. Müller escapes Germany unharmed, even though he is reported to be dead.

Glossary

communist
A person who believes that citizens should
  collectively own all property.

concentration camp
A work or death camp that kept thousands of
  people prisoner.

Final Solution
The planned elimination of European Jews by the
  Third Reich between 1941 and 1945.

Gestapo
The German secret police (*Geheime Staatspolizei*)
  formed by the Nazi government; the branch of
  the SS responsible for undercover espionage
  against enemies of the Nazis.

Holocaust
The term used to describe the deaths of millions of
  Jews and other civilians in World War II.

interrogation
The questioning of a prisoner.

Kristallnacht
The "Night of Broken Glass," November 9–10,
1938, when the Nazis rampaged throughout
Germany, destroying Jewish businesses
and synagogues.

plebiscite
A vote by which an entire nation or country
expresses an opinion for or against a
proposal or ruler.

putsch
An attempt to overthrow a government; a coup.

Reichstag
The German congress, in which elected officials
made laws.

Schutzstaffel (SS)
The private Nazi army, of which the Gestapo was a
part, also known as Black Shirts.

Sicherheitspolizei
The security police. A small government group
that worked outside the SS.

Sturmabteilung (SA)
Known as the storm troopers, or Brownshirts. The SA was a kind of private army working for the Nazis. It often was used to intimidate enemies and fight with the police and communists.

Treaty of Versailles
The treaty that ended World War I and imposed harsh terms on Germany.

Wannsee Conference
A meeting held on January 20, 1942, in the Berlin suburb of Grossen-Wannsee, and which formalized the Final Solution.

For More Information

Simon Wiesenthal Center and Museum
 of Tolerance
1399 South Roxbury Drive
Los Angeles, CA 90035
(800) 900-9036
Web site: http://www.wiesenthal.com

Survivors of the Shoah Visual History Foundation
P.O. Box 3168
Los Angeles, CA 90078-3168
(818) 777-4673
Web site: http://www.vhf.org

United States Holocaust Memorial Museum
100 Raoul Wallenburg Place SW
Washington, DC 20024-2126
(202) 488-0400
Web site: http://www.ushmm.org

Web Sites

The American Experience: America
  and the Holocaust
http://www.pbs.org/wgbh/amex/holocaust

Anti-Defamation League
http://www.adl.org

The History Place: World War II in Europe
www.historyplace.com/worldwar2

Holocaust Memorial Center
http://www.holocaustcenter.org/holocaust.shtml

Rutgers University
Holocaust Resource Center (Center for the Study
  of Jewish Life)
http://www.jewishstudies.rutgers.edu/hrc.html

Yad Vashem: The Holocaust Martyrs' and Heroes'
  Remembrance Authority
http://www.yad-vashem.org.il

For Further Reading

Browder, George C. *Hitler's Enforcers: The Gestapo and the SS Security Service in the Nazi Revolution.* New York: Oxford University Press, 1996.

Butler, Rupert. *An Illustrated History of the Gestapo.* Osceola, WI: MBI Publishing Company, 1993.

Crankshaw, Edward. *Gestapo: Instrument of Tyranny.* New York: Da Capo Press, 1994.

Douglas, Gregory. *Gestapo Chief: The 1948 Interrogation of Heinrich Müller.* Los Angeles: R. James Bender Publishing, 1995.

Emmerich, Elsbeth, and Robert Hull. *My Childhood in Nazi Germany.* New York: Bookwright Press, 1991.

Kallen, Stuart A. *The Nazis Seize Power, 1933–1941.* Edina, MN: Abdo Publishing Co., 1994.

Leapman, Michael. *Witness to War: Eight True-Life Stories of Nazi Persecution.* New York: Viking Penguin, 1998.

Sulzberger, C.L. *World War II.* New York: American Heritage, 1985.

Index

A

Allies, 63, 78, 84

Aryans, 33

assassination attempt on Hitler, 78–79

Austria, 67

B

Bavaria, 9, 14, 15

Bavarian state police, 17

Berlin, 36, 41, 48, 81, 89, 93

Bormann, Martin, 86

Braun, Eva, 86, 87

Britain, 24, 25, 63, 75

C

Communist Party, 20, 54

communists, 11, 17, 30, 32, 35, 41, 45, 56

concentration camps, 12, 30, 35, 44, 64, 65, 66, 70, 71

counterespionage, 42, 44

Czechoslovakia, 67

D

Dishner, Sophie (wife), 17

E

Eichmann, Adolf, 69

Enabling Act, 28

F

Final Solution, the, 66–67, 68

France, 24, 25, 63, 72, 73, 74

Führer, 28, 33, 59

G

ghettos, 64, 65, 67

Gleiwitz border incident, 5–8

Goebbels, Paul Joseph, 29, 86

Göring, Hermann, 31, 39

Greece, 67, 73, 74

Grünspan, Herschel, 36

H

Hess, Rudolf, 32

Heydrich, Reinhard, 13, 40, 41, 48, 65, 70

Himmler, Heinrich, 13, 40, 48, 68, 70

Hindenburg, Paul von, 28

Hitler, Adolf, 8, 19, 23, 25, 26, 28, 29, 31–33, 39, 42, 43–45, 50, 66, 70, 78, 79, 81–83, 86–92

Hungary, 67

I

interrogation methods, 57–60

Iron Cross First and Second Class, 15

Italy, 49, 73, 74

J

"Jewish Question," the, 64
Jews, 29, 32
  extermination of, 13
  Hitler's beliefs about, 33–34
  treatment of, 12, 33, 34–36,
    38, 65, 66, 70–71, 72

K

Kristallnacht, 36, 38

L

Lebensraum, 32
Leipzig, 36

M

Marxists, 45
Mein Kampf, 32
Müller, Elizabeth (daughter), 17
Müller, Reinhard (son), 17
Müller's escape from Germany,
    94–95
Munich, 15, 17, 19, 20, 41
Munich police force, 15

N

Nacht und Nebel Erlass (Night and
    Fog Decree), 67
Nazi(s), 8, 19, 20, 22, 23, 25, 28,
    29, 31, 32, 36, 39, 41, 43,
    45, 48, 50, 51–54, 57, 58,
    71, 75
Nazi Party (National Socialist
    Workers' Party), 19, 23,
    25, 26, 28, 29, 41, 42
Nuremberg, 36
Nuremberg Laws, 34

P

plebiscite, 28
Poland, invasion of, 8, 63, 65
propaganda, 29, 31, 54, 86, 87

R

Rath, Ernst von, 36
Raubal, Geli (Hitler's niece), 79
Reichstag, 20, 23, 26

S

Soviet Union, 47, 63, 67, 97
Spain, 73, 91
spies, 18, 19, 43, 44, 49, 75, 76,
    98, 99
SS (Schutzstaffel), 13, 39, 40, 41,
    64, 81
Stauffenberg, Colonel Claus von,
    78, 79, 80, 81, 82
Stuelpnagel, General Karl
    Heinrich von, 74
swastika, 29

T

Third Reich, 31, 36, 38
torture, 61–62
Treaty of Versailles, 19, 23–25

U

United States, 24, 63, 75, 97, 99
U.S. Army Counter Intelligence
    Corps (CIC), 89, 97–98

W

Wannsee conference, 68
Weimar government, 19, 20, 23, 25
White Rose, 73
World War I, 14, 19, 20, 23, 33
World War II, 8, 12, 63, 88

About the Author
Mark Beyer is the author of more than fifty books for young adults and children. He lives with his wife Lucy in New York City.

Photo Credits
Cover photo © Deutsche Presse-Agentur GmbH; p. 4 map by Claudia Carlson; p. 7 © Debra Gierach, courtesy of United States Holocaust Memorial Museum (USHMM); p. 10 © Estelle Bechoefer, courtesy of USHMM; p. 20 © Joanne Schartow, courtesy of USHMM; p. 24 © Popperfoto/Archive Photo; pp. 27, 34, 37, 46, 94, © National Archive, courtesy of USHMM; p. 30 © Harry Lore, courtesy of USHMM; p. 40 © Ullstein Bild; p. 52 © courtesy of USHMM; p. 56 © Bildarchiv Preussischer Kulturbesitz, Berlin 2001; p. 61 © Muzem Niepodleglosci, courtesy of USHMM; p. 66 © Marvin Springer, courtesy of USHMM; p. 71 © FPG International, LLC; p. 74 © Franklin D. Roosevelt Library; p. 80 © Corbis; p. 90 © Express Newspapers/Archive Photo.

Series Design
Cynthia Williamson

Layout
Les Kanturek

GAYLORD M